raise for ICONIC PRODUCT DESIGN

this age of accelerating complexity, it is a pleasure
e introduced to Wolfgang's beautifully illustrated
k—to just settle back, smile, and be reminded of the
forgotten, simple objects that we live with and enjoyed
in the past, present, and future."

—Charles W. Pelly, former president of
the Industrial Designers Society of America
and founder of BMW-Designworks

"An amazing time travel machine! This inventory of the
iconic objects of our daily life is a reference for all of us,
but also for our design schools and their students."

—Maurille Larivière, cofounder and president
of The Sustainable Design School, Nice, France

"This collection is a timely reminder that not everything
has been digitally transformed. Talented human beings,
designers who care passionately about the people who will
use their designs, continue to inspire. Form-making that
will become iconic the way these are is not easy; but worth
learning how. This is an exceptional guide in the quest."

—RitaSue Siegel, founder and partner,
RitaSue Siegel Resources

"Amazing how he has illustrated the everyday products
we use that have become the symbol and representative
image in our minds for a whole category of products,
e.g., Carousel Projector, Apple MacIntosh, Walkman.
Design is global."

—Dana Wolcott, adjunct professor
and lead innovation coach at
Rochester Institute of Technology

ICONIC PRODUCT DESIGN

An Illustrated History
of the World's Most
Innovative Devices

Wolfgang Joensson

Skyhorse Publishing

Skyhorse Publishing books may be purchased in bulk at special discounts for sales promotion, corporate gifts, fund-raising, or educational purposes. Special editions can also be created to specifications. For details, contact the Special Sales Department, Skyhorse Publishing, 307 West 36th Street, 11th Floor, New York, NY 10018 or info@skyhorsepublishing.com.

Skyhorse® and Skyhorse Publishing® are registered trademarks of Skyhorse Publishing, Inc.®, a Delaware corporation.

Visit our website at www.skyhorsepublishing.com.

10 9 8 7 6 5 4 3 2 1

Library of Congress Cataloging-in-Publication Data is available on file.

Cover design by Wolfgang Joensson

Print ISBN: 978-1-5107-5778-3
Ebook ISBN: 978-1-5107-6162-9

Printed in China

Contents

Acknowledgments

"It takes a village to write a book" was the exasperated advice from my sister-in-law, Dr. Cindy Ott, a fine author and professor of American history. Her entertaining, yet instructive writing style has been a leading example for me. She is right to point out the necessity for help from others, which is why I would like to thank her and the following people for their support and help.

First in line is Ian Ferris, a brilliant designer who came up with the idea that I should write and encouraged me on my way. Several of my designer friends have motivated and helped me choose the icons: Tim Toomey, Dieter Wanke, and Ronald Ihrig. My business partner, Lutz Gebhardt, discussed with me and also contributed icon ideas. His unwavering support and enthusiasm is just one of those life forces everyone should have around.

Having designed but never written before, I relied heavily on the patient support, editing, criticism, and overall inspiration of my muse and partner in life, Susan Kuntz. Her relentless will to drop everything and discuss my book was highly appreciated throughout the process. From the very early pages on, she has diligently worked with me on the content and made sure the result is presentable. Without her, this book—and my life—would not be half as good.

Jim Peterson and Jonathan Duff, both great writers, have helped me to understand writing better, and I thank them for their time and effort. John Flint, a former editor, has helped me tremendously by suggesting reading material to improve my writing and advising me on how to make my text better. He has also painstakingly edited everything.

As a designer, I want to create all visuals by myself, but I am smart enough to know when to ask for help there, too. Urs Stemmler, a great transportation designer, helped me with ideas and criticism regarding some icons. Angelika Scholz, as often in my past, once again gave me advice on typography. The architect Jon Schultz has enthusiastically helped from the start with tasteful advice to improve contents and design.

My gratitude also goes to my editor, Nicole Frail of Skyhorse Publishing, who has diligently edited my writing, researched for verification, and corrected mistakes I made. You helped a great deal to make this book perfect.

Last but not least, a big thank-you to my brilliant agent, Fran Black from Literary Counsel, who is the best agent any writer could have: supportive, highly professional, perfectly organized, and a lovely person.

This is the village of my friends, and I consider myself lucky to have them.

Design Creates Memories

Do you remember the first product you bought for yourself? That Sony Walkman for listening to your favorite music? Or the Swiss Army knife you got as a present from your uncle? Can you recall your mother making cake with the KitchenAid mixer? Such products keep us company from the cradle on. Some even find their way into our memories—and our hearts.

This book is about personal relationships with objects, but it is also about the impact designed objects can have on us as a society. Every one of them contains meaning: cultural, historic, social, or emotional. For example, when several German mineral sources get together and decide to have a unified bottle to be more visible on the market, this becomes important for public health, since their product competes with less healthy sugar-based soft-drink choices. To have a common package design makes their product more visible next to international sweet-drink giants.

What makes a product iconic is a common response based on individual feelings. Without emotions, there are no icons. Although emotions are personal, when many people react in the same way, their judgment provides a common ground for evaluation.

I use the term iconic in a different way from linguists or semiologists. A strictly scientific approach to design is insufficient, for designers also care about emotions, and that can rarely be done in a systematic or predictable way. Nor can their approach be called purely artistic, for they also care about function, production, and how the product will find its way into the hands of a customer. It is this duality that makes design such an exciting activity. Blending function and form demands an understanding of emotions as well as logic and science.

Every serious designer aims to create objects that endure the test of time, become coveted and influential. Iconic products are even more valuable—if not directly, then by the value they add to the brand they represent. SONY, for example, has never been more fashionable than during the high time of the Walkman, a product coveted by everyone, but particularly youngsters.

Since I started to work as a designer, I have been interested in what makes design appealing, noteworthy, and, most of all, memorable. There are many good ideas and pretty shapes, but it takes more to make an icon. It is fascinating to see how the designers on the following pages shaped our surroundings and improved our lives through the creation of innovative objects of beauty and desire.

What Makes Products Iconic?

Iconic products are memorable, and to be memorable, they have to stand out and be different. More than that: they have to be better than the rest. What makes products superior and anchors them in our minds is either an innovation or a content to which we can emotionally respond. With these two components, a product can become an icon—a representative of a category, of an era, or of a spirit.

Havaianas are the ubiquitous sandals. These flip-flops have come to stand for beach life—and not only in Brazil. They evoke summer, care-free times, minimalism, and basic comfort.

Only quintessential products give you the feeling you are seeing not just a lamp, for example, but *the* lamp—if not the top-quality one, then perhaps the one with the most advanced technology, or the one that makes you do a double take and think, *This one is special*. You feel it.

This is an emotional response to a successful communication between the designer and you. When it is shared by many people, the product has attained "iconicity."

How does that happen? There are two main avenues: to imbue the product with emotional content, or to stimulate by innovation. Emotional content can be based on function, while innovation tickles our curiosity and arouses desire.

Understanding the user is the key to any design solution. After a new product has been produced and marketed, it has to be sold, but most important, it will be used. This is where human expectations come in. Before we consider a purchase, we look at the object. We try to read it. We expect hints about function, but we are also open to an emotional appeal. We like to like.

As users, we want stuff that works and that we understand. We also want to enjoy the products we buy as long as possible. In other words, we want practical, intelligible, quality products.

Intelligible design helps us see how something works. We appreciate a sophisticated product, but we must be able to understand it. We want to know where the top and the bottom is and how to open, refill, or maintain it. We users need clues. A remote control is useless if we cannot change the batteries when they are dead.

We want quality. But without consumer feedback or expert advice, we have to rely on whether the product looks solid. The real factors that influence sturdiness—the type of material, wall thickness, and construction—are not usually obvious. Expression of quality becomes as important as quality itself.

Aside from making users feel good about a product by matching their expectations regarding its reliability and longevity and assuring them that they do not need to read an instruction manual, what can be done to delight their senses? Understanding of provenance and respect for the environment, if communicated well, incite a positive emotional reaction with everyone. With provenance, I refer to where the product was build, and by whom. The country of origin and the brand that represents the circumstances of production is something we associate with values—something we can relate to. Respect for the environment does not only include sustainability, which people have come to expect; it also means the environment where the product will be sold—we shop differently online from in a boutique, a supermarket, or a high-end department store. And we feel differently about those choices. Every product exists also in a historical context, and if we see the time we live in reflected by the design, then this makes us feel good. And whenever we feel good, chances are greater that we remember it.

New things attract us, but so do familiar ones. Market research shows that user groups tend to prefer the well known, so for new designs, acceptance is always an uphill battle. That means that designers shouldn't copy existing solutions, but create designs that provide orientation by using proportions, shapes, or details we know. Successful design provides visual clues about the product, but it avoids borrowing an identity from something that already exists.

How to make something new? More important: how to make something better? Innovation is the solution—to apply an existing principle to a new area. Whereas invention makes new use of the laws of physics, innovation is invention's little sibling and easier to plan. A designer can have three new ideas by next Thursday about how to dispense coffee into a cup. Coming up with new ways to make coffee instead is not that easy. For its manageability, its appeal to people, and its power to impress, innovation is paramount.

Innovation exists on various levels. An alarm clock with a glass cover for travel is a neat little innovative idea. Sometimes the main function is innovative. When the product starts a new category, like a smartphone, then the entire product is innovative. Innovation can also be visual—and should be. Great ideas have to be discernible. When you add a corkscrew to a pocket knife, show it. Then it will be understood and will sell—the prerequisite for becoming useful and adopted.

Form should communicate function. If one is new, the other has to be, too. In most iconic products, however, form and function are both innovative, for function is not only technical: a toaster not only browns bread but is also part of the morning ritual, the home decor, and maybe a celebration when gifted.

There are no appearances without significance or connotation, and our perception of forms is influenced by everything we have seen before. New or familiar, every form means something. It is the designer's responsibility to ensure that the form he chooses expresses the meaning he wants to convey. Form is much more than "just a shape"—in the words of the French writer Victor Hugo, it is contents rising to the surface. There is always a relationship between what something is and what you see. Form is anything but superficial: it is profound. At least, to be iconic, it has to be.

Communication through form between designers and users of an object is neither obvious nor self-evident. Our emotional responses as users to visual stimuli are individual and, of course, subjective. Design is not science. We cannot measure design, but that makes it only more exciting and challenging. The most important phenomenon in life escapes such quantification—emotions. And though you cannot calculate them, they count. Emotions are the reason why there are no fail-safe paths to make people understand a design. This makes the examples in this book so impressive: these designers managed somehow to leave a note understood by many. Remembered over time, that is what made them iconic.

Iconic Product Design

One of the earliest examples of industrial design. Produced for centuries in Stoke-on-Trent, this British teapot combines remarkable functionality with an archetypical design. Made of Staffordshire clay, which is said to retain heat particularly well, it features a non-drip spout and a bulbous form that allows the tea leaves to swirl and steep properly. Every detail has proven for generations to produce the best possible tea, an intrinsic part of British lifestyle. The unchanging brown glaze serves to hide tea stains and looks good after generations of use. The designer of this plain but robust object, as well as its name's origin, remain unknown.

Brown Betty Tea Pot
Great Britain 1695

Come hell or high water, these boots will keep your feet dry. The first Duke of Wellington had no idea what would happen when, in the early nineteenth century, he told his shoemaker to improve the boots worn by Hessian soldiers. Decades later, a businessman bought the rubber patent from the tire maker Charles Goodyear, made those boots waterproof, and opened a French company to manufacture Wellington Boots. The so-called "Wellies" were particularly appreciated by soldiers trying to prevent trench foot on the battlefields of World War I. Combining a rugged outdoor style and the cachet of adventure the Wellies continued their success around the world.

Rubber Boots
France 1852
Hiram Hutchinson (American-British)

How to make a curvaceous sculpture from a tree?
Cut it into strips, lathe them, then bend those over
steam around a form. The result is ingenious and an
example of beauty and practicality. Unassembled,
three dozen chairs fit into a single box. To allow
spilled liquids to drain quickly, woven cane
material was used for the seat. This made it perfect
for Austrian coffee houses, hence its nickname
Wiener Kaffeehausstuhl. At a time of mostly one-
off furniture, this one was notable for its serial
production process. No other product better marks
the beginning of industrial design.

THONET
Chair No. 14
Austria 1859
Michael Thonet (German-Austrian)

To contain fizzy liquid without losing pressure, you need a tight seal. In this bottle, a glass marble pushed up by the pressure of the carbonation does the trick. The red rubber ring and the glass intuitively express that function. To pop the top, you merely had to push down the marble with your thumb. Only problem was kids loved to smash the bottle and play with the marble.

HOPE GLASS WORKS
Mineral Water Bottle
United Kingdom 1873
Hiram Codd (English)

A bottle with dimples makes it easier to grasp when pouring a dram or two. This functional advantage also gave character and a strong image to this elegant form, so much so that the brand of whiskey sold in the bottle adopted Dimple as its own name. It is distinctive also as being the first bottle shape to be patented in the United States.

DIMPLE
Whiskey Bottle
Scotland 1890
unknown

Fold it away. That's what you can do to reduce the risk of cutting yourself with an open knife blade. Add a corkscrew to open that bottle of wine, and you have a very practical and extremely versatile tool. A limitless variety of models has been launched, but the basic idea remains—a useful, handy, and quality utensil right there in your pocket.

WESTER & CO
Pocket Knife
Germany 1890
unknown

A pleasing ergonomic handle, sculpted from wood, a simple twist-lock, *et voilà!*—a tool so emblematic of French culture that it has become the generic name for any wooden-handled knife. Unchanged for more than a century, this vital utensil is found not only in many households, but also in workshops of craftsmen and artists. Even Pablo Picasso sculpted with it, proving that perfection can be truly inspiring.

OPINEL
No. 10 Knife
France 1897
Joseph Opinel (French)

The brush feels soft in the hand, and its smooth curves make it easy to grasp. The flexible red-rubber cushion holds the bristles—an innovation labeled "pneumatic" by the creator. Almost unchanged from the original design and still available well over a century later, this is proof that no better brush has ever been conceived. The shape's simplicity is striking, giving it a timeless elegance.

MASON PEARSON
Hairbrush
United Kingdom 1885
Mason Pearson (English)

When banks sought to improve employees' efficiency by creating a better work environment, the time was right for an American engineer to create a lamp with a shade as green as the visors of the money-counters. The direct light cast around the lamp's base, together with the soft glow of the emerald glass shade manufactured by specialists in Moravia, is easy on the eyes. It creates the perfect atmosphere for reading and writing and has therefore become popular in libraries, offices, and homes.

EMERALITE
Desk Lamp
United States of America 1909
Harrison D. McFaddin (American)

With its combination of feminine curves and phallic profile, this is probably the most recognizable shape in the world. It is also the first bottle ever to be patented. With a form that evolved over many iterations, it always kept the characteristic emblematic shape, embodying a sensuality that made it distinctive.

COCA-COLA
Coke Bottle
United States of America 1915
Earl R. Dean (American)

Almost a century old and nearly unchanged, this product combines a robustness with a design that evokes familiarity and conviviality. You see where the motor sits. The stand swings protectively around the bowl. Easy to understand and ready to mix, it blends ingredients, but it also blends into the kitchen environment.

KITCHENAID
Mixer
United States of America 1918
Herbert Johnson (American)

Although the first telephone booth was erected in Berlin in 1881, it is the British version that has become more evocative. Its design draws on visual imagery from architectural artifacts like tombs and galleries in London. With a dome-shaped roof, intricate paned window structure, and bright-red color, the booth has become synonymous with the British capital and English culture. Even if you've never been to London, you've surely seen them in the movies.

K2
Phone Booth
United Kingdom 1920
Giles Gilbert Scott (English)

The glass sphere gives a warm glow—that's comfortable.
Light is directed to the desk it stands on—that's practical.
The choice of glass and chrome—that's modern. This lamp
represents the Bauhaus design style (basic geometric
forms, material honesty, and serial production) in an
exemplary way. Its purity is striking, even today.

Table Lamp
Germany 1924
Wilhelm Wagenfeld (German)

When a student's work gets instant recognition, it must be exceptional. It is even more astounding if it is someone's first creation, like this remarkable teapot with infuser, made from silver and ebony. This exceptionally gifted photographer, artist, sculptor, and designer created it shortly after joining the Bauhaus. Her outstanding career at this famous Weimar design school did not end with her diploma. She went on to become acting workshop director—and negotiated some of the most important contracts between the school and industry. She ultimately left, moved to Berlin, and became head of metal design in a factory, where she continued to produce outstanding work.

Tea Pot
Germany 1924
Marianne Brandt (German)

French love their food and their women, so it should not be surprising that they charmingly refer to this casserole as a *cocotte*: an endearing word for women in general but also for *une belle-de-nuit*, a girl-of-the-night. Available in multiple colors, its production is solidly hand-finished and its design almost unchanged since its inception. Many unforgettable meals, lovingly prepared and served in it, have certainly contributed to its iconic status.

LE CREUSET
Dutch Oven
France 1925
Octave Aubecq (French), Armand Desaegher (French)

For furniture to be useful, it must be versatile. This pioneer of interior design and architecture wanted her creations to be multifunctional. She developed this ingenious little side table for her self-designed house in the south of France. She made it height-adjustable to use while in bed or when sitting in one of the iconic fauteuils she designed during her illustrious career. Its materials, steel and glass, were revolutionary at the time and created an elegant and lightweight object for her home. In a time when it was difficult for women to succeed professionally, she left an indelible mark with her outstanding work.

Table E 1027
France 1927
Eileen Gray (Irish)

The time must have been ripe. Three designers—Mart Stam, Le Corbusier, and this one—had similar ideas almost simultaneously of how to improve seating comfort. All three capitalized on the metal tube's flexibility and resiliency to create a chair that rocks slightly. It feels softer than the material suggests, bouncier than typical four-legged chairs. This model was not the first but became the most successful, probably because the combination of industrial steel with traditional woven cane makes it versatile for office as well as dining, and it looks sleek even today.

THONET
Cantilever Chair
Germany 1928
Marcel Breuer (Hungarian)

The future never seemed closer nor more desirable than in the early thirties of the last century. Coming out of the Great Depression, people embraced technology with a romantic fervor. Everything had to be aerodynamic. The winds of change certainly influenced the shape of this product. The creator, an industrial design pioneer, created a practical item here, which was also an excellent representative of an era focused on style.

Iron
United States of America ~1930
Walter Dorwin Teague (American)

Long before World War II, and decades before German designers devised soft-lined, clear-cut products, an exceptionally talented former Bauhaus staff member created this beautifully simple table clock for the company she headed. With a series of household items comprising bookends, napkin holders, and ashtrays, she showed her genius with a no-nonsense approach. Her legacy was established with her exceptional metal work as a student, but she continued to deliver beautiful objects until the war, and later, the socialist economy of East Germany put an unfortunate end to her design career. She continued to work as an artist, but it is regrettable that she could not express her expertise in more design objects.

RUPPELWERKE
Table Clock
Germany 1930
Marianne Brandt (German)

What you see is what you get. With a visible and
adjustable infusion, true tea lovers can prepare their
brew exactly as they like. All it takes is removing the glass
sieve filled with tea leaves in time. The design's rigorous
restriction to one material speaks of purity yet is soft and
evocative in its shape. Total transparency is achieved with
elegance and panache.

SCHOTT
Tea Pot
Germany 1931
Wilhelm Wagenfeld (German)

You want a highly adjustable desk lamp that remains in position once fixed in place? This auto mechanic used his knowledge of car shock absorbers to create a product that is functional, practical, and comfortable to adjust. He and his business partner also created the name. The lamp has so much character and personality that an animation company chose it for its company logo.

Anglepoise Lamp
United Kingdom 1932
George Carwardine (English)

Whatever the weather, this baby will light your fire. A great invention that made our lives simpler and more comfortable, just as the zipper that inspired its name. This solid product works reliably in any conceivable adverse condition. Launched just before World War II, it won a place in the pockets and hearts of countless military and civilians. Thanks to its serviceability and strong build, it is still on the market today.

ZIPPO
Lighter
United States of America 1933
George G. Blaisdell (American)

Disseminate propaganda! This was the secret objective that brought this radio into people's homes. A deceptively simple loudspeaker box, it communicated its purpose unwittingly. The blend of Bakelite with a woven loudspeaker cover and the rounded edges softened its appearance in an attempt to integrate it into the home. Successful and insidious.

DR. G. SEIBT
VE 301 W ("People's Receiver")
Germany 1933
Walter Maria Kersting (German)

Nowadays, we talk into devices that look like flat bricks, but in the early days, in order to determine the perfect ergonomic angle between the mouth and earpieces of telephones, this design office measured hundreds of people's heads. With those measurements, they created the first phone-to-house ringer and network circuitry, based on an Ericsson model created by the Norwegian artist Jean Heiberg. By the standard of those days, it provided good acoustic quality. Collectors lovingly refer to it as the Lucy phone, a common prop from *I Love Lucy*, the popular 1950s sitcom.

WESTERN ELECTRIC
302 Phone
United States of America 1936
Henry Dreyfuss (American)

To highlight the colors and quality of the glaze, this company's design director used stepped concentric circles. With this quintessential product of the Art Déco period, you could set a festive table with a variety of pieces in a range of colors. During World War II, the product line was disrupted because the source of the red-color version was uranium, which caused concern about radiation as well as its need for the war effort. The manufacturer then lost faith in the product and discontinued production for more than a decade. The whole line was relaunched in 1985 and is seeing a strong revival today as a retro design.

HOMER LAUGHLIN CHINA CO.
Fiestaware
United States of America 1936
Frederick Hurten Rhead (English)

"You push the button, we do the rest!" This manufacturer's slogan was targeted at people who liked photography to be simple. The name of this model, featuring a smooth body in pure Art Déco design, emphasized lightweight construction and sturdiness. Raised lines provided just the right grip on the otherwise smooth metal surface. Nothing distracted from the focus of easy operation, which proved the slogan to be true.

KODAK
Bantam Special
United States of America 1937
Walter Dorwin Teague (American)

When fire destroyed the stock of this Cologne luggage manufacturer—all except the aluminum raw stock—the owners turned disaster into success. The result was a lightweight suitcase fashioned from this metal. With sturdy outside ridges, which gave it high stability, it evoked the progressive aviation age. The company continued to innovate and in 2000 introduced the first suitcase with two polycarbonate shells zipped together, still with the same identifiable ridges to maintain its strong brand image.

RIMOWA
Aluminum Luggage
Germany 1937
Richard Morszeck (German)

Thumb-sized, this camera was still tightly packed with sixty patented inventions by the engineers. The result was practical and easy to use, particularly for covert operations against an enemy. Originally a precision instrument with new camera technology made entirely from metal, it lost its luxury appeal over time. With an increasing amount of plastic parts and the low-resolution images provided by its tiny negatives, it could not compete with better-performing modern devices. That was the end of this model.

MINOX
Riga Camera
Latvia 1936
Walter Zapp (Latvian)

The original patent for Morgan Parker's two-piece scalpel
dates to 1915. When it expired, this British manufacturer
refined and perfected the tool. The simple ergonomic
shape and surface pattern convey its function. That
unmistakable and distinctive image has become
synonymous with its use in surgery as well as for arts and
crafts. With this product, its manufacturer became the
world leader it still is today.

SWANN-MORTON
Scalpel
United Kingdom 1937
unknown

Spare, yet very expressive, the strict form of this espresso maker renders the process intuitive. When you fill it with water and heat it on a stovetop, the water will boil and expand. This pushes the hot water upward, through the sieve with the coffee grounds in the middle of the device. Steam pressure then forces the espresso to rise to the top. The company's owner recognized the iconic status of his famous product, requesting that his remains be stored in one for his funeral ceremony.

BIALETTI
Moka Express
Italy 1933
Alfonso Bialetti (Italian)

This manufacturer's name means "people's car," and it was promoted as such. Families collected coupons that allowed them to purchase it, but many cars were never delivered due to World War II. Once the war was over, it became the most popular car in Germany, and soon in the entire world. After many years, it continued to stand out because the manufacturer stuck to its form while competitors had moved on. Cuddly and with big headlight "eyes," it aroused parental instincts in its owners. Technically, it was an exercise in frugality and practicality, with a famously reliable air-cooled engine. A journalist compared the car to a "little shiny bug" when it was launched, and the nickname "beetle" stuck.

VOLKSWAGEN
Beetle
Germany 1939
Ferdinand Porsche (Austrian-German)

To help his wife, a hairdresser, furnish her new salon, this young metalworker built three sturdy, practical trash bins, operated by a foot pedal. A win at a raffle later enabled him to invest in manufacturing his bins industrially. Popular in doctors' offices, its hygienic hands-free opening mechanism also appealed to private households and sales soared. The still family-owned company offers a range of products, all in only one version, following a philosophy of creating an "essential" product that fits in many homes and "has a chance to last a very long time." The onomatopoetic company name mimics the sound of the lid closing, but is also the Danish word for the seesaw mechanism of the pedal opening.

VIPP
Pedal Bin
Denmark 1939
Holger Nielsen (Danish)

After visiting a Modern Arts exhibition in Paris, this talented illustrator and stage designer ventured out and focused on product design. To boost American morale toward the end of the 1930s Depression, he created this patriotic radio for the manufacturer's fiftieth anniversary. Using modern plastics and production processes, he devised a cheerful object that echoed the American flag. With stripes like Old Glory and stars on the volume and station knobs, it had red, white, or blue loudspeaker grilles and handles. Among the many impressive product and transportation designs created by this outstanding representative of modernist design, the aptly named Patriot Radio stands out as evocative and inspiring.

EMERSON RADIO & PHONOGRAPH CORP.
Patriot Radio
United States of America 1939
Norman Bel Geddes (American)

This founder's son traveled to America during the 1929 Wall Street crash. Sensing an opportunity, he decided to produce luxury lighters, catering to clients not affected by the crash. The first ones were produced in aluminum, since the more resilient brass was a strategic material restricted to war purposes. The lighter became known for its outstanding quality. For some time in the sixties, all lighters from this company were made of eighteen-karat gold, with a small percentage of brass. Sleek lines and geometric decorative patterns made it one of the most socially acceptable men's jewelry pieces of the time.

S. T. DUPONT
Lighter
France 1941
unknown

A box with a hole pretty much describes the original brownie camera in 1900. It took a little more time to become the emblematic product named after the Brownie cartoon character created by Palmer Cox. Easy enough for children to use and robust enough for soldiers to take into battle, it became a line of simply constructed and inexpensive cameras. Suddenly anyone could become a photographer. Artistic people saw the camera's potential, and together with some of the photos taken with it, the camera itself became iconic.

KODAK
Brownie Six-20
United States of America 1946
unknown

Every clock shows the time. This one not only displays
the actual hour and minute, but it also shows the time of
its genesis—the postwar (WWII) era. It reflects people's
desire to have fun again. With numerals playfully replaced
by brightly colored spheres, this instrument magically
changes from a device that conveys precision and
reliability to one engendering a lively mood with hope for a
more promising and brighter future.

HOWARD MILLER
Ball Clock
United States of America 1947
George Nelson (American)

"The only truly original and beautiful design for such an object"—so said the photographer Edward Steichen. Minimalism personified, it needs only two hands and an orientation (here provided by a slightly concave polished twelve o'clock disk) to show you the time. An impressive reduction, a testament to the creator's talent.

MOVADO
Museum Watch
Switzerland 1947
Nathan George Horwitt (American)

How does one transport a basket filled with raw eggs
on a bumpy country road without breaking them? The
creative briefing was a challenge, but the car's innovative
suspension met it with élan. With unsurpassed practicality
and a shape that raises emotive responses, it is arguably
the car that most deserves to be included in a lineup
of iconic products. Its value-retention is amazing, too.
Originally developed to make farmers more mobile, it
has since been driven by generations of people, with or
without eggs.

CITROËN
2CV
France 1948
Flaminio Bertoni (Italian)

Early cathode tubes for television sets were round. The image displayed on them was square. The challenge: to find a good compromise between those extremes. This one met that challenge with a beautifully sculpted form, reminiscent of Art Déco architecture. Emphasis on ventilation slots provides an architectural look like a power station, while the dark-colored casing draws attention to the screen.

BUSH
TV 22
United Kingdom 1948
unknown

Nothing speaks more of summer and backyard barbecues than this archetype of grills. An inspired worker in a marine buoy factory turned the two parts of a buoy into the prototype of today's well-known product. Refined continuously over the years, its rounded shape efficiently contains heat and is easy to clean. A sturdy wheel base makes it mobile for use in the yard or garden.

WEBER
Grill
United States of America 1950
George A. Stephen (American)

Fountain pens blot. Newspaper ink is more viscous and dries faster than regular ink. In 1938, László Bíró turned this observation into a pen with patented ball mechanism and sufficiently viscous ink. Marcel Bich (the company name is a simplified version of his) and his partner Édouard Buffard bought the patent. They developed this pen, which today is the world's best seller with more than 100 billion sold. With its simple, ergonomic shape, it does not roll off the table and is known for affordable quality.

BIC
Cristal Pen
France 1950
Décolletage Plastique (French)

For Italians, when making coffee, the result is what counts.
The preparation can become a ceremony. Resembling a
miniature factory, this machine promises and produces
rich espresso with low caffeine content. Its high-quality
appearance is due mostly to the polished chrome surface,
which announces: expect the best!

PAVONI
Europiccola
Italy 1950
unknown

You want to be a star? Not so easy—but looking like one is. Don these shades and you're halfway there. Comfortable to wear, the shape—neither too rounded nor too edgy—is easily recognizable. Ubiquitous use by movie stars has made the black-rimmed lenses with the small almond-shaped detail synonymous with fame.

BAUSCH & LOMB
Ray-Ban Wayfarer
United States of America 1952
Raymond Stegeman (American)

Good enough for Eric Clapton and Buddy Holly. With a two-tone, contoured shape and three pickups (a first) for richer sound quality, it was created to enable people to play and enjoy music better. Many instruments evoke an era or a musician, but this one merits a mention on anyone's short list. The fame of many great players has rubbed off on it.

FENDER
Stratocaster
United States of America 1954
L. Fender, B. Carson, G. Fullerton, F. Tavares (all American)

This "magic stick" (English translation of Zauberstab)
turns you into a culinary wizard in no time. So perfect was
the original construction that only a few small changes
have been made since its launch. The recognizable
ergonomic silhouette of this reliable device has won a
place in the kitchens of professionals and passionate
amateurs alike.

ESGE
Zauberstab
Switzerland 1954
Acton Bjørn (Danish)

Close your eyes and think of England! If you see a red double-decker bus, then you may have the same steadfast appreciation for tradition as the Brits. To go from Oxford Circle to Piccadilly, all you had to do is hop on the rear platform. Its characteristic vertical outline makes it one of the most recognizable city vehicles in the world.

LONDON TRANSPORT
Routemaster
United Kingdom 1954
A.M. Durrant, Colin Curtis, Douglas Scott (all English)

It's so easy to dismiss a bowl as being just a bowl! This product, however, does the job right—enough to become memorable. A little handle and a small spout, and (since the sixties) a rubber foot to reduce slippage. Made of temperature-tolerant thermoset plastic, the hard surface is nearly scratch resistant, unlike cheaper versions in thermoplastic material. It features a rounded inside for easy whisking and vertical walls to save space in the fridge.

ROSTI
Margrethe Mixing Bowl
Denmark 1954
Sigvard Bernadotte (Swedish), Acton Bjørn (Danish)

Do you dream of flying through Italy with a partner sitting behind you? You need a motorized two-wheeler to share the joy. There are lots, but this one has made it into the hearts of scooter enthusiasts. Its image is universal, evoking dreams of vacations in the land of *la Dolce Vita*.

PIAGGIO
Vespa
Italy 1946
Corradino d'Ascanio (Italian)

No fairytale character is buried in this radio/record player combination despite its nickname of "Snow White's coffin." But this radical departure from the old style of home audio equipment does mark an end of an era. Only the wooden sides are reminiscent of the previous style, where radios looked like furniture. The modern appearance, with bent perforated steel, reflects a change in music taste in postwar Germany to include jazz and rock 'n' roll. The plexiglass cover protects the record player and dials. It's also the reason for the nickname.

BRAUN
SK 4
Germany 1956
Hans Gugelot, Dieter Rams (both German)

It sounds paradoxical: hide the bulb, but let the light shine through. Curved metal sheets in a sophisticated arrangement make it possible. The overall impression is one of complexity, yet lightness. The creator—an architect—was inspired by a vegetable. He left his mark by designing whimsical lamps like this one.

LOUIS POULSEN
Artichoke Lamp
Denmark 1958
Poul Henningsen (Danish)

You wanted to be in here—at least if it
was the rolling index (hence, rolodex) of
an important person. A Danish engineer
working in New York had the idea of
facilitating access to the addresses of
one's business contacts. The result
was so popular that its name became
generic—a dream of every company and
one of the hallmarks of iconicity.

ROLODEX
Address File
United States of America 1958
Hildaur Neilsen (Danish)

No, it's not an iPod, though it does resemble the audio entertainment device launched half a century later. This product was manufactured by one of the most design-oriented companies of its time, a radio manufacturer founded by a mechanical engineer. It set standards in brand image continuity, including graphic design of its instruction manuals, packaging, and product design. No wonder today's designers and brands are still inspired by their early peer's efforts.

BRAUN
T3
Germany 1958
Dieter Rams (German)

This speaks Bauhaus: no decorative pattern, basic geometric forms. Yet despite their clarity and rigor, the tools never compromise at the expense of the user. Their ergonomic design and dishwasher-friendly stainless steel marked a new age in dining culture. Every modern set of cutlery descends from this bold statement of purism.

MONO
A
Germany 1959
Peter Raacke (German)

Stackable china is a good idea, taking less cabinet space at home and in restaurants. This robust professional tableware could withstand abuse, which was also an advantage in your kitchen. Its innovative modular system with plates, cups, bowls, jugs, and creamers was originally conceived for public tables, but it was also popular in private households. It's still available today.

THOMAS
TC100
Germany 1959
Nick Roericht (German)

TV sets were not always portable. In fact, this was
the first. It also had a revolutionary look. Instead
of a square box surrounding the tube, the housing
continues the tube's shape to the back. The mobility
and futuristic style set it apart from the competition.
Considered at the time a luxury product, its success
was unfortunately compromised by its price, and so
it didn't sell well.

SONY
8-301
Japan 1959
unknown

A legless chair, elegant, stackable, made from one piece of material. This could only be done with the development of modern plastics. At first, it was manufactured from polyester, reinforced by hand-layered glass fiber—more artisanal than industrial. After considerable investment in molds, it was then produced in polystyrene, which reduced the sales price. To improve the chair's longevity, polyurethane foam was subsequently used. Finally, polypropylene made it even more affordable. All versions spoke to the possibilities of appealing plastic furniture with a flowing organic shape.

VITRA
Panton Chair
Switzerland 1960
Verner Panton (Danish)

A magic drawing board that can be used forever.
A stylus displaces gray powder on the back of a
screen. One knob moves the stylus horizontally,
the other one vertically. The lines remain—until
you shake the box and the powder coats the
screen anew. Developed by a French technician,
it was named the most popular drawing toy of
the twentieth century.

OHIO ART COMPANY
Etch A Sketch
United States of America 1960
André Cassagnes (French)

Some ideas are so simple. A hole for a broomstick makes it easier to lift the heavy marble base of this lamp. The creators, two architect brothers who preferred common sense and straightforward design, were inspired by streetlights. A two-part lampshade allows light to be directed where needed. It appeared in an iconic James Bond movie, which accelerated its path to fame.

FLOS
Arco
Italy 1960
Achille & Pier Giacomo Castiglioni (both Italian)

Accuracy in a watch is rather important. Here for the first time, instead of a balance wheel, a tuning fork keeps the rhythm. This watch shows off its supreme technical innovation right on its face. Visible workings on the front made it notable and heralded its position in the vanguard of timekeeping.

BULOVA
Accutron
United States of America 1960
unknown

A golf ball that writes. Letters arranged on a small sphere were pushed against the ribbon to mark the paper. By replacing the ball, you could change the fonts. This new technology brought flexibility to typing, a first step toward desktop publishing. The generous futuristic curves of the machine reflected the innovative level of the product and helped inspire those sitting in front, writer's block or not.

IBM
Selectric
United States of America 1961
Eliot Noyes (American)

How to package a key ingredient of Japanese cuisine? This gifted Japanese designer mastered the challenge. He created a modern bottle that expressed the ancient heritage of liquid containers. The simple form pleases. A smart detail—the double spout—lets you pour from either side, and the size of the spout nibs allows you to control how much you want and how fast. The red cap's color evokes traditional oriental lacquer techniques and their predominant color scheme.

KIKKOMAN
Soy Sauce Bottle
Japan 1961
Kenji Ekuan (Japanese)

Blenders have to stand rock solid. This one not only does that, but it also looks the part. The angle of the cone-shaped base facilitated extraction from the mold during production, an important constraint in the early days of plastic household appliances. Its profile speaks of stability, power, and efficiency and has been sold for longer than half a century.

BRAUN
MX 32
Germany 1962
Gerd Alfred Müller, Robert Oberheim (both German)

Shaving your face is supposed to be a manly activity, so these designers created a masculine grooming device with this black razor—previous models were as pale as soap. They also made in-depth ergonomic studies and created multiple wooden models that ultimately led to this shape. When the perforated patented foil head touched the face, beard stubbles passed through the holes and were cut off. Sharp blades never touched the skin, which resulted in a close, smooth, and superior shave.

BRAUN
Sixtant SM 31
Germany 1962
Hans Gugelot, Gerd A. Müller (both German)

To go barefoot in summer is fun, but risky—your feet may need protection. These sandals provide as close to a barefoot feeling as you can get. They promise relaxation, vacation, and no worries. Originally created for the Brazilian soccer team (hence the national colors) these instantly recognizable shoes say "beach!" in every detail. No longer popular only in South America but worldwide, they are now available in a panoply of colors and patterns. Planned as inexpensive shoes and sold for fifty cents, they can now be found priced for dozens of dollars.

HAVAIANAS
Flip-Flop Sandals
Brazil 1962
Robert Fraser (Scottish)

Who doesn't love 3D images? Since 1839, people have been fascinated by stereoscopy, and this extends to today, when virtual-reality glasses provide the same experience with moving images. This 3D slide-viewer was initially made of Bakelite. After the introduction of lightweight thermoplastic, it became cheaper to manufacture, easier to handle, and gained success worldwide.

VIEW-MASTER
Model G
United States of America 1962
unknown

Show and tell. From the sixties to the nineties, no presentation by an ad or design agency was conceivable without the use of this slide projector. The magazine contained 80 or 140 slides, which was sufficient to visually explain complex scenarios to an audience. Magazines could easily be switched, and presentations using several carousels could be projected in parallel. This was a forerunner to today's computer multimedia presentation.

KODAK
Carousel
United States of America 1963
Hans Gugelot, Reinhold Hacker (both German)

The die is cast. At least it was when these two brilliant designers worked on a portable radio. It consists of two hinged parts. When the colorful shells are opened, they display controls and the loudspeaker. When closed, the carrying handle and the antenna retract, and the resulting shape is round and smooth all over.

BRIONVEGA
Cubo Radio
Italy 1963
Richard Sapper (German), Marco Zanuso (Italian)

Smudged ink is messy; it stains your sleeve or blotches your document. That dilemma impelled this company's president to invent the felt-tip pen, the first one to use this technology. Liquid ink is directed to the tip through fibrous material, with the benefit that it dries much faster than ink from a fountain pen. With the same design for over half a century, the body has a hexagonal section to prevent it from rolling off the table. Simple and efficient.

PENTEL
Sign Pen (Fiber Tip Pen)
Japan 1963
Yukio Horie (Japanese)

Here's looking up at you! This TV set makes it easy to view even when positioned on the floor. That was important for young college kids or first-time homeowners who might not have had all their furniture yet. The cuddly rounded shape, frameless tube, glossy and brightly colored plastic housing, and quirky antennas all spelled cute and friendly. A flexible and mobile solution for people who moved often.

BRIONVEGA
Algol 11
Italy 1964
Richard Sapper (German), Marco Zanuso (Italian)

Two billion personal computers are in use in the world today. This is their ancestor—the first programmable desktop computer. It did not have a screen. Results were printed on a roll of paper and data memorized internally or on a magnetic card. Marketed as the more familiar "calculator" to overcome fears of potential users, it had neither integrated circuits nor microprocessors, since they were not yet available. Previous computers were as big as wardrobes. The architect who designed this model used the opportunity of a smaller size to create a personal object.

OLIVETTI
Programma 101
Italy 1964
Mario Bellini (Italian)

When a designer couple visited a manufacturer producing plastic Mickey Mouse ashtrays, they wondered: "Can't you make something better?" Their answer was a stackable, dishwasher-proof dinnerware system that maximizes use of space while providing an elegant, minimalist solution to dinner table settings. Everything nests smartly in the next larger item. Vertical walls ensure neat stacking. An American manufacturer bought the molds from the meanwhile bankrupt Italian company and produced a line in white and subsequently in rainbow colors. The creators added many pieces like bowls, covers, and trays. Their sustainability credo, "if you do it right, it will last forever," was prescient—the current manufacturer plans to produce them "forever."

ARTICOLI PLASTICI ELETTRICI
Stackable Melamine Dinnerware
Italy 1964
Lella + Massimo Vignelli (both Italian)

Making hard materials look soft is the source of this lamp's appeal. Any good desk lamp directs light where needed. This one uses very few parts and is bent in a way that fulfills the task with minimum effort. No extraneous parts just for show—this is decorative minimalism at its best.

O-LUCE
Spider
Italy 1965
Joe Colombo (Italian)

A bulb within a bulb—what a concept for a lamp. This one is truly representative of the Pop Art era. It ironically enlarges the shape of a mundane light bulb and repeats the image inside with a real one, all to create a lamp nonetheless. It is the product of a creative genius who successfully navigates between art and design. Although mass-produced, it can still be considered a piece of art. That alone makes it notable.

STUDIO M
Bulb Lamp
Germany 1966
Ingo Maurer (German)

Where are those scissors? Even if you live alone, you probably misplace yours at times. Orange handles make these easy to spot. They are the best-known product of a company that started as a foundry in 1649 and that produces steel and steel products from axes to steam engines. There's even a left-handed version, as the enhanced ergonomics are dexterity-sensitive.

FISKARS
O-Series
Finland 1967
Olof Bäckström (Finnish)

We typically take pictures to capture moments. That's why the process should be easy. This company always focused on making photography simple: point and shoot. The model's uncluttered design looks as simple as picture taking should be. A new film format, supplied in cartridges loadable in broad daylight, and a rotating cube with four flash bulbs, made sure it was. This product opened the market even more for consumers who wanted to record visual souvenirs without having to get technical.

KODAK
Instamatic
United States of America 1968
Kenneth Grange (English)

Good package design reveals what's inside.
The little raised bubbles mimic the sparkling
water in this bottle. Together with the waist,
they also improve the grip. To compete with
soft-drink giants, German water sources unified
the packaging for their mineral waters with this
bottle. Produced by the billions, it's difficult to
imagine how this design could be improved.

GDB
Mineral Water Bottle
Germany 1968
Günter Kupetz (German)

A light switch should be as simple as possible, but not any simpler. You shouldn't have to be Einstein to switch on the light, after all. This designer reduced the form language to the extreme: cable and housing are round, the switch itself square. This nicely emphasizes the importance of the process with a design that remains in the background.

VLM
Light Switch
Italy 1968
Achille Castiglioni (Italian)

Keep calm and drink tea—and make sure your teapot is as serene as the experience. Here, one material and one color harmoniously unify the elements. Glossy and matte surfaces separate handle and spout from the main corpus. The goal of the Bauhaus founder and architect was to subtly indicate, but not overly emphasize, the different functions of the various parts.

ROSENTHAL
Tea Pot
Germany 1969
Walter Gropius (German)

Sometimes the best ideas come when you're on the move. This product was advertised as "for all places except the office," and people loved its transportability as much as its round shape and glossy red plastic. It needed the advent of modern plastics to turn the mundane typewriter into a fun tool. Mobility was enhanced by a collapsible grip on the back and a cover from which the typewriter emerged, as if from a drawer.

OLIVETTI
Valentine
Italy 1969
Perry A. King (English), Ettore Sottsass (Italian)

Originally conceived as a toy to teach children about geometric shapes, this practical poster-sized silo for utensils is a design classic that adorned households and offices in the seventies. When her own children showed no interest in the toy, the creator, who had no training but an obvious gift for design, started to think of other uses. Her inspiration came from childhood memories of her father's drugstore and photo shop. Its abundance of drawers and a hanging toiletry bag gave her the idea of storing things vertically. With her husband, she invested in expensive tooling. The product became a huge success and remained the most popular of all iterations she later developed.

DESIGN M
Wall Storage Panel
Germany 1969
Dorothée Becker (German)

A hair dryer does not have to look like a gun, though early hair dryers often did. They were also bulky and, if made of metal, had safety issues. When this company began to produce a new line of appliances in plastic, it challenged standardized shapes. Dryers typically consisted of a motor, a vertical handle, and a horizontal air outlet. This easy-to-hold model has both air intake and outlet on the front, which results in a smaller package and better portability.

BRAUN
HLD 4
Germany 1970
Dieter Rams (German)

A bull in a china shop would have endless fun with
this four-person dinner set of nineteen pieces. Soup
bowls, main dish plates, and dessert bowls can all be
satisfyingly stacked to form a complete sphere. Glazed in
contemporary color schemes of the era, it is an excellent
example of usable pop art. The patented limited edition
was more an experiment than a product aimed at large
consumer groups. The ceramic worker and the daughter
of the company's owner who created this earthenware
masterpiece later modified its shape and used melamine
instead, making sets more suitable and practical for
camping or dining al fresco. The products are out of
production now but can be found at auctions.

VILLEROY & BOCH
La Boule
Germany 1971
Helen von Boch (German), Federigo Fabbrini (Italian)

Patience is a virtue. For those who didn't have it, there was Edwin Land. One of the last true inventors of our time, he developed instant photography so we no longer had to wait for the results. Surprised by the success of his first "polaroid" camera—a name alluding to the polarizing filters his system required—he still thought it too bulky. A paperback book size is what he had in mind. The result was this camera and the parallel development of color polaroid film, representing the pinnacle of his career.

POLAROID
SX-70
United States of America 1972
Henry Dreyfuss (American)

There was a time before computers when
television was our main electronic contact
with the outside world. With a nod to its role at
the center of many households, this designer
created a sculpture that was appealing from all
sides, including the back. Parts made by plastic
injection molding encased the working elements.
The creators gave users' emotional needs priority
over functional constraints and captured this in
the catchphrase "form follows emotion."

WEGA
TV 3050
Germany 1972
Esslinger Design (German)

Nobody likes cables. Although electric light was a boon to mankind, we can do without the stringy hassle. Here, low voltage is conducted through the two bars that hold the head, insulated by red plastic elements at the hinges. Instead of springs and complicated mechanisms, the lamp head is balanced with counterweights. It lends an image of serenity to this beautiful object, which is reinforced by its smooth movement.

ARTEMIDE
Tizio
Italy 1972
Richard Sapper (German)

Form interacts with function. This provides the interest and appeal of this lamp. It consists of a bent tube with a weighted steel wire threaded through it. The weight keeps the steel string taut, and because of the bend, there is friction that keeps the tube from sliding down the wire. The lamp, which sits on the tube, can easily be adjusted to any height just by moving it up and down.

FLOS
Parentesi
Italy 1972
Achille Castiglioni, Pio Manzù (both Italian)

How to protect a portable calculator from potential environmental hazards? By completely encasing it in rubber, including the keys. Even the electronics inside are protected, making them impervious to accidental liquid spills. With a look like no previous calculator, it readily communicates that this is an innovative idea.

OLIVETTI
Divisumma 18
Italy 1972
Mario Bellini (Italian)

A simple, little, but magical idea—a light box. Closed, it's off. Open, it's on. Clever and puzzling. The light can be directed with the reflective lid. You always wonder: when closed, is it really off? And how does it know?

CINI & NILS
Cuboluce
Italy 1972
Franco Bettonica, Mario Melocchi (both Italian)

One and one is two. But what is 7,568 divided by 0.3492? No need to think with this portable calculator in your hand or pocket. After mechanical, electric, and then electronic ones, this device represented a giant leap in its field and took only a short time to dominate the market. With higher precision than a slide ruler and much easier to use, this early model captivates with the organization of keys, display, and function switches. A protective clear cover clips on the back.

DENNERT & PAPE
Aristo M 65
Germany 1972
Rainer Behnisch (German)

This fits in the fist, and with its soft curves and smooth surfaces, it easily slips into our pockets. It is designed to keep us company. The brand known for its pens decided to branch out into disposable lighters. The result, created by a brilliant and versatile designer, became immediately popular. With a smooth red surface for the push-button valve and a knurled texture for the starter wheel, the indications of functional parts are clear and simple.

BIC
Lighter
France 1973
Louis Lepoix (French)

This watch sends signals. The protruding yellow, blue, and red spheres to stop and adjust time show this watch is different. They're also easier to twist. But there is more. The asymmetrical design allows more freedom of movement for the wrist, since the watch rides higher up the arm. Traditional watch materials were abandoned in favor of aluminum and rubber. A high-contrast watch dial completed the new look.

LIP
Dark Master
France 1973
Roger Tallon (French)

One of the early electronic watches, this timepiece was designed for the lower price market in both kit and assembled versions. It provided unparalleled accuracy, even when compared to very expensive mechanical watches. The face featured a clear separation into three horizontal areas. The top one housed the display. The middle one had a button hidden under soft plastic left and right, to show time or count seconds. The bottom gave access to replace batteries from the back. With just a black plastic strap and red LEDs, it had a touch of the mysterious and magical.

SINCLAIR
Black Watch
United Kingdom 1975
Clive Sinclair (English)

You like music. Why should you be bothered with technical complexity? With eight buttons on the remote to control volume or choose your music station (or record player), here is a simple interface between user and product. It makes the life of audio aficionados easier without compromising quality. The two Danish engineers who founded the company understood there are consumers who love music but not electronics. They perfected how you interact with the device, hiding functions less used under a panel next to the touch buttons on the receiver.

BANG + OLUFSEN
Beomaster 2400
Denmark 1976
Jacob Jensen (Danish)

Some like it hot. And to keep your liquids that way, this product does the job, thanks to an ingenious lid. It pivots to let the steaming coffee out when you incline the carafe to pour but swings back to close when you set it down. All that, thanks to gravity and smart design. And that little black dot on the side? It's the visible part of the inner mechanism that holds it in place. It also indicates the pivoting point of the lid, for visual feedback.

STELTON
Thermal Carafe
Denmark 1976
Erik Magnusson (Danish)

What you see is what you get. Clean, simple lines with few parts. The lightbulb is half covered by a silver-colored reflector that directs it downward. A cage around it protects the user from touching the hot metal. The fitting has a switch, the cable hangs free, and the hinged steel rods allow for easy angle adjustment. Simple bent steel profiles are easy to produce but provide for a fully functional and adjustable lamp with character. This production method allows for extending the brand to wall-hanging, standing, and desk models.

ARTEMIDE
Sintesi
Italy 1976
Ernesto Gismondi (Italian)

This product has its priorities straight. The revolutionary idea behind this receiver/amplifier/ tape recorder/record player combination lies in the rigidity of the layout. Buttons, dials, and switches have been laid out in a grid. Vertical separation divides functions assigned to each component from left to right. Horizontal areas are arranged according to the frequency of their use. Main buttons are placed closest to the user, readouts being farthest away. This helps audiophiles who want all options at their fingertips but without confusion.

WEGA
Concept 51K
Germany 1978
frogdesign, Hartmut Esslinger (German)

Let there be light. But also here. And there. This designer created a lamp that shines down, provides diffuse light around the center, and ever-so-slightly reflects some of the light upward. With admirable simplicity, he just added a suspended disk with a hole. Illuminating us in more than one way, this lamp is testimony to the talent of its creator.

FLOS
Frisbi
Italy 1978
Achille Castiglioni (Italian)

A message in a bottle. It reads: perfect for an active lifestyle. Optimum choice of materials—hygienic plastic for the mouthpiece, reliable silicone rubber for the seals, and lightweight aluminum to reduce the weight—makes it ideal for energetic activities. Right down to the detail that lets you open it with your mouth while on the run.

SIGG
Water Bottle
Switzerland 1978
Kurt Zimmerli (Swiss)

Afraid of the dark? Whether you are or you need your flashlight only for emergencies, you want to be able to rely on it. This outstanding lamp is rugged, easy to use, ergonomic, and reliable. Made of high-grade anodized aluminum, it features a krypton or xenon light source for the adjustable beam. The product has brought solid comfort to security forces and private citizens alike.

MAGLITE
Flashlight
United States of America 1979
Anthony Maglica (American)

Come rain or come shine, with these shades you are prepared. You can swing up the nose bridge and exchange lenses to adapt to various light conditions. Using aviator sunglasses developed for the Air Force of the United States in 1936 as a model, this design company created a modern version with replaceable lenses. They wrap comfortably around the head and protect against glare but also disguise a good part of the face if you want to go incognito.

CARRERA
Sunglasses
Austria 1979
Porsche Design (Austrian)

It's a relief to find a public toilet when you need one. This is a hygienic space to answer the call of nature—an intricate, free-standing container that cleans itself after each use. The looks are rugged and neutral, but sufficiently textured to discourage vandals, reassure citizens, and blend into any urban environment.

JCDECAUX
Public Toilet "S.P.E.A."
France 1980
Jean-Claude Decaux (French)

A tape recorder that does not record? The
marketing department originally resisted.
No wonder it took years before the idea—
to wire a hifi amplifier to a simple cassette
tape mechanism—took hold. Yet this little
device changed our lives by enabling us to
listen to music in high fidelity on the go.
And for a while, it imbued the brand with a
youthful spirit.

SONY
Walkman
Japan 1981
Sony Design Center (Japanese)

Get a grip. This razor invites you to hold
on tight with soft rubber dots protruding
its stainless-steel shell. Not only do the
dots give it a unique character, but they
also stand for the patented shearing foil
system of the shaving head. Innovative
in technology and design, this product
established the standard for shaving devices
and for product quality in general.

BRAUN
Micron Plus
Germany 1981
Roland Ullmann (German)

Life is an adventure. This versatile tool lets you deal with unexpected incidents. Inspired by pocket knives, the creator expanded on the idea by adding pliers. The quality of build, precision, and material choice of this versatile tool make it exceedingly popular. Surprisingly, this company is named not after the sturdy leather pouches its tools come in, but after one of the founders.

LEATHERMAN
Pocket Survival Tool
United States of America 1982
Timothy S. Leatherman (American)

You can see right through it because it's plastic. When some Swiss members of the watch industry developed the idea of a plastic analog watch, they turned the market in their favor. With heavy investment in injection molding and ultrasonic welding, and using half the pieces of a comparable watch, they managed not only to reduce the production price to a fraction, but also to offer high-precision watches in a range of styles. Although this model was not the company's first, it most beautifully displayed the new plastic technology by its transparency, something classic watches could not do.

SWATCH
Jelly Fish
Switzerland 1983
unknown

A little friend on your desktop. The company
founder himself insisted on a screen closer to the
front, as he did not like the screen's frame looking
like "furrowed brows" hanging over it. The device's
frontal appearance, deliberately proportionally
different from other personal computers, showed
its innovation level. From its graphic user interface
to the mouse, it heralded industry firsts. It's hard to
understand how paradigm-shifting this design was,
but it was indeed revolutionary.

APPLE
Macintosh
United States of America 1984
Steve Jobs, Jerry Manock, Terry Oyama (all American)

You want to hear when the water is ready for your beverage. Here, a triple pipe announces the boiling point harmoniously. With a steel body and a plastic handle to protect from the heat, this kettle is a visual statement. In the mid-eighties, an array of designer kettles suddenly appeared on the market. Very few were as clever as this one.

ALESSI
Bollitore
Italy 1984
Richard Sapper (German)

How did people communicate before mobile telephones? Today, we can hardly imagine what life was like without this brilliant technical innovation. When this company produced the first commercially available mobile phone that deserved the name, it was the beginning of an era. The design emphasized that everything—battery, antenna, receiver, and all the works—was self-contained. Though a little bulky by today's standards, it was compact.

MOTOROLA
DynaTAC 8000x
United States of America 1984
unknown

Whatever your sport, when you exercise fast, your eyes
need protection. This designer and businessman started
manufacturing grips for motorcycle handlebars in a soft
plastic material he patented and called Unobtainium.
Looking for wider opportunities for innovation and
earnings, he developed goggles for athletes that featured
nosepieces made from his material. Thus, sports
sunglasses were born. When the first American winner
of the Tour de France wore these yellow-framed glasses,
both became instantly famous. The creator's company
(named after his dog) continued to push innovation, new
materials, and complex geometries to optimally cradle the
human face. His brand grew to become a household name,
coveted in the world of sports and by the military.

OAKLEY
Factory Pilot Eyeshades
United States of America 1984
James Jannard (American)

Who likes to be awakened by an alarm?
Nobody. At least this novel idea made
the process of getting up easier. All you
had to do was shout "Stop!" when it
rang, and it went quiet. No fishing for
the clock, no leaving the warm pillows.
This provided a new comfort level and
quality of interaction. The trademark
clarity of the dial, the fine details, and
the practical protective cover made it
a perfect travel accessory, since it was
small enough to pack, but big enough
not to get lost.

BRAUN
AB 312 vsl
Germany 1985
Dietrich Lubs (German)

No heavy metal, all lightweight aluminum.
Polished profiles hide the spring mechanism.
The lampshade and the bulb fitting are finished
in matte aluminum. Restriction to one material,
subtle variation in surface treatment, simple lines
combined with excellent functionality. That's all
one needs in a lamp.

ARTEMIDE
Tolomeo
Italy 1986
Michele De Lucchi, Giancarlo Fassina (both Italian)

Take note. If you want it to be permanent, you had better use this marker. Graffiti artists, restaurant owners, company managers, teachers, scientists, and children have all chosen this pen for their distinct needs. Its popularity is testament not only to the quality of its tip and ink, but also to its size, proportion, and cap. Using empirical research, the designers developed the most ergonomic and easiest way to uncap it by creating little ribs, which also prevented the cap from rolling off the surface.

EDDING
Marker 3000
Germany 1987
Jens Plewa (German)

This is the real thing. You have probably seen this design on your smartphone screen because it inspired interface specialists generations later. They adapted its design and layout for virtual calculator keyboards on computers and mobile devices. For the original, the designers, after numerous experiments, determined concave buttons were best for a keyboard like this. The systematic application of subtle colors and the fine detailing of the housing were masterful.

BRAUN
ET66
Germany 1987
Dietrich Lubs, Dieter Rams (both German)

Light is more than waves and rays. For more than a hundred years, straight cones were used to indicate the physicality of light, which is a logical idea. This designer went metaphysical. He chose a cornucopia as a metaphor for the richness that light brings into our lives. Tipping the horn, which swivels on the pole, cleverly switches the light on and off.

FLOS
Ara Lamp
Italy 1988
Philippe Starck (French)

Not all of us live in a yellow submarine, but who wouldn't want to? Whether this tape player reminds you of maritime warning colors or of underwater vehicles from pop songs, its bold design, functional water protection cover, and rubberized buttons invite you to bring it along on the boat or to the beach. Most likely only a few of these were immersed in water, but the suggestive design hinted that you could if you just wanted to.

SONY
Walkman Sports
Japan 1988
Sony Design Center (Japanese)

Whether you wanted to chase an Italian plumber through a mushroom kingdom or precisely stack Russian building blocks without using a TV, you had to have one of these handheld devices. The Japanese company that made them was founded in the 1800s as a manufacturer of playing cards. It branched out into the electronic gaming world in the early 1970s, eventually becoming a worldwide success with the improved ergonomics of the so-called D-pad design (its trademark cross-shaped direction button) and removable cartridges for different games. Within two weeks of the product launch in Japan, all Game Boy units sold. Today, more than one hundred million devices have been scooped up by enthusiastic consumers. Nintendo consoles still dominate the handheld gaming market.

NINTENDO
Game Boy
Japan 1989
Gunpei Yokoi (Japanese)

Designing for the elderly benefits us all.
Not only because we all hope to get older,
but because better ergonomics are always
an advantage. This smart design uses
soft silicone to provide a nonslip grip and
a comfortable place for the thumb while
peeling, making us all feel better about
this mundane task. Planned for a small
market segment, it enjoyed surprisingly
broad success. The principle has since been
applied to a wide range of kitchen gadgets.

OXO
Peeler
United States of America 1990
Smart Design (American)

Does form follow function? And if so,
which function? An excellent example
of functionality's various meanings,
this product made its designer famous
and its manufacturer rich. In addition
to its juicer function, it could serve
as a very decorative present. In other
words, it worked well on several levels.
It almost seems too much to ask it
to separate the seeds from the juice,
which it doesn't.

ALESSI
Juicy Salif
Italy 1990
Philippe Starck (French)

Regular vacuum cleaners collect dirt in bags. This outstandingly talented designer and engineer was unhappy with their effectiveness once those bags started to fill up. He applied his considerable engineering skills to improving how they work. Replacing the costly bag, which clogs up, he used a canister in which the impelled air rotates. The centrifugal forces separate the lighter air from the heavier dust. Emptying the canister is all the user has to do. The bold color scheme and expressive geometric shapes—never before seen on a household appliance of this size—effectively communicated the innovation.

DYSON
DC01
United Kingdom 1993
James Dyson (English)

Should products have personalities? Absolutely.
Should they look like little people or creatures?
Why not? This product was among the first of many
gadgets where the function and its expression
were not enough—at least in the eyes of the
creator and the manufacturer. Whether that is
appropriate depends on if you see this primarily
as a bottle opener or, more important, as a fun
accessory to celebrate happy times. The name
of the product and the hairstyle of the character
are references to a colleague and friend of the
designer, Anna Gili.

ALESSI
Anna G.
Italy 1994
Alessandro Mendini (Italian)

A fun computer. Why? Because computers could be more than tools for the office; they could also provide entertainment. After the Macintosh was established as a truly personal computer for the home and work, the Internet arrived, and with it all the fun websites, online gaming, and access to information. To acknowledge our increasing use of computers for pastime pleasures, this company dared to be bold. Transparent housing in a range of lively colors let us peek inside. It was not just a pretty face, since it could provide the performance necessary to fulfill any task. It was also the company's first product with an 'i,' denoting its easy Internet access, but also referring to individual, imagination, and innovation.

APPLE
iMac
United States of America 1998
Jony Ive (English)

A bike with smaller tires needs an improved suspension. This brilliant engineer invented a rubber cone suspension system for his friend Alec Issigonis's minicar. Then he developed several bicycles that also featured rubber suspension and small wheels. Improving the frame, he extended it sideways and labelled it Spaceframe. The resulting construction was compact, but lightweight and stiff and looked different. It had an architectural quality.

MOULTON
Spaceframe Bicycle
United Kingdom 1998
Alex Moulton (English)

We want information at our fingertips, or in the palm of our hands. Preceding smartphones, personal digital assistants (PDAs) like this one paved the way for mobile electronic organizers. A must-have for professionals, they contained calendars, address files, and messages. Among the many models, this one stood out due to its technical specifications. The metal housing included an integrated rechargeable battery. The anodized aluminum shell looked sleek and was more scratch-proof than previous plastic models.

3M
Palm V
United States of America 1999
IDEO (American)

You have to pull some strings to get this player working. An amazing idea—no buttons on this exemplary minimalistic CD player, just a loudspeaker. Simply pull the power cord; the motor spins and the disk plays until the cord is pulled again. This designer knew exactly how to make a music device fun, whimsical, and intuitive. The loudspeaker pattern gave it enough visual interest to be familiar, yet not boring.

MUJI
CD Player
Japan 1999
Naoto Fukasawa (Japanese)

Immortal—mobile phones from this company had a reputation for being indestructible. The unique exchangeable shells meant you could replace them when they got scratched, and you could customize. A range of colors and surfaces was available. In spite of the double walls that the shells created, it was also quite slim and easy to handle.

NOKIA
8210
Finland 1999
unknown

Meant for a quiet day at home. The first desktop computer without a ventilator, it featured a silver metal cube floating in a plexiglass "cage." CDs ejected vertically in a rather theatrical way. Using a touch-button main switch just added to the feeling of effortlessly efficient electronics at your fingertips, perfect for home, office, and private use alike.

APPLE
Cube
United States of America 2000
Apple Design Team (American)

Carry all your songs in your pocket. This small package could hold days of music. With the company's newly created music software, the way we consume music was turned upside down. Easy and fast download of songs from the largest record companies for a standard fee, combined with the ability to arrange titles into "playlists" and listen on the go —that was revolutionary. The inspiration for the design clearly came from Braun's earlier radio models, as the designer freely conceded. Obviously, he shared the idea that nothing should distract from the experience.

APPLE
iPod
United States of America 2000
Jony Ive (English)

Comfortable as a throne for a king, reminiscent of centuries-old shapes. Few designers can pull that off in transparent, injection-molded plastic. Improving the ergonomics of the era pieces by creating a very pleasant seat and adding stack-ability are proof of the designer's mastery. Who would think plastic could be so comfortable? When asked, he responded: "I don't like to sit on a corpse"—dramatically exaggerating his turning away from designing chairs upholstered with leather.

KARTELL
Louis Ghost
Italy 2002
Philippe Starck (French)

Humans are mobile and smart. Why shouldn't their phones be, too? When this computer company entered the mobile phone market, people queued up to snatch one of the first samples. The aura and reputation of the company accrued to its unknown product. Today, after several iterations, the phone itself has achieved iconic status, thanks to its quality, versatility, and uncompromising minimalism. Rather than designing an object that draws attention to itself, the goal was obviously to create a perfect frame, an ideal canvas for all types of content appearing on it.

APPLE
iPhone
United States of America 2007
Apple Design Team (American)

Education is vital for every society, but developing countries are often held back by lack of access to information. That is why a Greek-American architect thought of equipping every Third World child with a computer. A price tag of $100 ensured affordability, while a "buy two, donate one" program emphasized his goal. Designed to be rugged and versatile, the initial model even featured a crank to generate electricity in the device, but it was later replaced by a more efficient charger. The designer created an object so iconic that its image can be found on Rwandan banknotes. The friendly-looking, practical device has been sold by the millions.

OLPC
Laptop for Children
United States of America 2007
Yves Béhar (Swiss)

The second mouse gets the cheese. This one gets admiration for its perfection. When the inventor Douglas Engelbart came forward with his idea for a pointing device, he could not have guessed its roaring success. After mechanical capture, laser optics now do the job. Buttons have been replaced by a surface that pivots for clicking and serves as a touch pad at the same time. The surface is smooth with extraordinarily improved functionality. Amazing construction quality, with a metal injection-molded bottom and battery cover, completes this magical device.

APPLE
Magic Mouse
United States of America 2009
Apple Design Team (American)

In the eye of the storm, the air is calm. This fan—
labeled "air multiplier" to underline its innovative
technology—features a big hole where normally
the blades would be. Few companies are pursuing
innovation with such fervor. From the more
powerful, yet more silent motor to the original
airflow, every detail has been reconsidered and
improved to blow all similar products away. The
result is a new and spectacular object. Its design
has a sculptural quality and visual impact that is
not only on a par with the technology, but strongly
communicates it.

DYSON
Air Multiplier
United Kingdom 2009
James Dyson (English)

Whether your tap water just tastes funny or contains organic contaminants, this bottle filters it as you drink. With a filter able to purify 300 times the bottle's contents, it is a practical and affordable product for quenching one's thirst. A filter change every two months is enough to ensure continuous purification to international standards. The squeezable flask itself is made of recycled plastic. Replacing the millions of discarded single-use bottles that will clog up the sea tomorrow is a brilliant and much more sustainable idea. The designer created a practical object in candy colors with a seductive shape, knowing that while we may want to save the environment, we have come to expect the process to be fun.

O2COOL
Water Filter Bottle "Bobble"
United States of America 2009
Karim Rashid (Egyptian-Canadian)

Do you remember old thermostats with unbelievably small numbers indicating the temperature? Then you know how advanced this product is. Design is not only about form—it's also about experience. Here you see how warm or cold it is, and how you programmed it. It's smart, but its intelligence is used to make it less complex. It hooks up to pretty much any modern heating or cooling system, integrating seamlessly with other devices like smoke detectors, webcams, or electric locks. You can remote-control your climate at home via an app. Best of all, it helps save energy and money. Making the whole device one giant rotary dial is logical and simple, but it was never done until this one came along.

NEST
Thermostat
United States of America 2011
Fred Bould (American)

One out of seven people in the world do not have access to energy. These two friends, an artist and an engineer, thought about the consequences. For education, you often need light after sunset. To climb out of poverty, you might need to work after dusk. This is why they developed "Little Sun," a solar-powered lamp that charges during the day and gives light at night. This makes the user's life safer, eliminating respiratory problems and fire hazard from smoking lamps and candles, as well as the environmental issues from the usage of torches. Light also reduces violence against women at night in refugee camps and is a source of empowerment. The palm-sized product can give up to 50 hours of light on a single five-hour charge. The social project delivers light where it is needed subsidized by the sales in stores around the world, as well as through donations.

LITTLE SUN
Solar-Powered Lamp
Germany 2012
Olafur Eliasson (Danish-Icelandic), Frederik Ottesen (Danish)

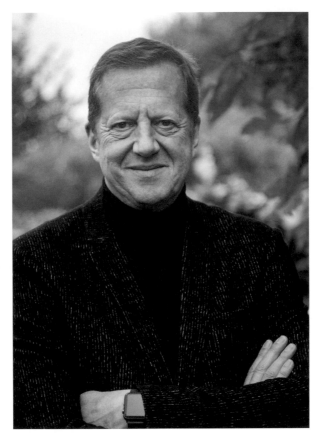

Photo: Juan Yuste, Madrid/London

About the Author

For nearly four decades, I have worked as a designer with start-ups like Hommage to multinational giants like Samsung, and on products ranging from rubber ducks to gas chromatographs. My creative credo? To make products easier to use and understand by designing them expressively. And, though beauty is a subjective concept, I care about it deeply. While I always hope my designs will become iconic, the closest I've come so far is having a coffee machine, which I designed for Switzerland's most valuable brand, JURA, in the largest German design museum in Munich.

I started my design career working with Pentagram in London and frogdesign in the Black Forest. In 1988, I opened my own design office, now VIEWSDESIGN, located in the Saint Germain des Prés area of Paris, where I work on product, interface, and brand design. My friend and partner Lutz Gebhardt runs VIEWSDESIGN Switzerland in Basel.

Simultaneous to my design work, I became an educator at age thirty-one when I was appointed chairman for product design at Art Center College of Design, on its European campus in Switzerland. After that, I was named Directeur des Diplômes at Strate College in Paris. During the same period, I became professor and department chair at a new Swiss design school, planning and running its product design department. I also taught design management at universities in Solothurn and Zürich, and at the International Management Institute in Lausanne.

Being a teacher is a mind-set, not an occupation, as much as a school is not a house, but individuals sharing knowledge. Design has to explain and to inspire, and in my two decades of working in education, I have done the same, trying to enlighten and to stimulate young talents.

Through my engineer father and my arts and crafts teacher mother, I was exposed to scientific and artistic influence. As I was born in South Africa and have resided in Germany, the United Kingdom, Switzerland, South Korea, and California before moving to Paris, France gave me a broad cultural perspective. Picking up languages along the way, I discovered parallels between linguistic and design thinking. Shapes, details, and colors are vocabulary, and designing with these elements requires syntax and grammar, and this is how I communicate, by addressing emotions as well as the rational mind.

As much as design does and should speak for itself, there is information, background, and context that I feel worth sharing with people, which is why I decided to write this book.

List of Designers

List of Manufacturers

Bibliography / Sources

For this book, I have researched in books and online. The books I have used are listed below, without indication as to which page has provided information about which product.

Schnellkurs Design, Dumont 1995, Thomas Hauffe, ISBN 3-7701-3388-9

Le Design Book, Phaidon 2013, ISBN 978-0-7148-6696-6

Design heute, Prestel 1988, Volker Fischer, ISBN 3-7913-0854-8

Iconic Designs, Bloomsbury 2014, Grace Lees-Maffei, ISBN 9780-8578-5352-3

The Design Encyclopedia, The Museum of Modern Art 1994, 2004, Mel Byars, ISBN 0 87070 012 x

Researching online, I have used Wikipedia mainly for verification and will not list those articles here; also no websites from companies that produce or have in the past produced the respective product. Other websites with information pertaining to specific products are listed below, in chronological order of the product launch, as sorted in this book.

./. • Brown Betty Tea Pot • ./.
https://bit.ly/34GK1oC
https://bit.ly/2Vt3DRS
https://bit.ly/2XHBCbY

./. • Rubber Boots • Hiram Hutchinson
https://bit.ly/2Vt3NZu
https://bit.ly/3ad4AmA
https://bit.ly/3bfiF4o

THONET • Chair No.14 • Thonet Brothers
Le Design Book, Phaidon, p 018, ISBN 978 0 7148 6696 6
http://bit.ly/2BiOo1T
http://bit.ly/2rpFVdj
http://bit.ly/2DWMmr4

HOPE GLASS WORKS • Mineral Water Bottle • Hiram Codd
http://bit.ly/2Bjj7LY
http://bit.ly/2DWH3aW
http://bit.ly/2mZgt9X

DIMPLE • Whisky Bottle • unknown
http://bit.ly/2mWlDmd
http://bit.ly/2DnCMwe
http://bit.ly/2DuXSw7

WESTER & CO • Pocket Knife • unknown
http://bit.ly/2BjFYXT

OPINEL • No.10 Knife • Joseph Opinel
http://bit.ly/2F2Mvs7
http://bit.ly/2DviGED

MASON PEARSON • Hairbrush • Mason Pearson
   http://bit.ly/2EZXZg6
   http://bit.ly/ZpWeoo

EMERALITE • Desk Lamp • Harrison D. McFaddin
   https://bit.ly/3cn58aX
   https://nyti.ms/2Kcd1nz
   https://bit.ly/3eu5NsY

COCA-COLA • Coke Bottle • Earl R. Dean
   http://bit.ly/2qpeUBc
   http://bit.ly/2DyabYh

KITCHENAID • Mixer • Herbert Johnson
   http://bit.ly/2Bk9Aoa

K2 • Telephone Booth • Giles Gilbert Scott
   http://bit.ly/2noNz9p
   http://bit.ly/1n1986K

./. • Table Lamp • Wilhelm Wagenfeld
   https://bit.ly/2Vbo8n2
   http://bit.ly/2rqen7E

./. • Tea Pot • Marianne Brandt
   https://mo.ma/2VvSPT7
   https://nyti.ms/2xyPVVC
   https://bit.ly/2Vxtjgj

LE CREUSET • Dutch Oven • Octave Aubecq, Armand Desaegher
   http://bit.ly/2mZ8UjL
   http://bit.ly/2DyaiTH

./. • Table E 1027 • Eileen Gray
   https://bit.ly/3bdTOoV
   https://bit.ly/2XEXy7F
   https://bit.ly/2RHn4VM

THONET • Cantilever Chair • Marcel Breuer
   http://nyti.ms/1vXJApV
   http://bit.ly/2mZAMUL
   http://bit.ly/2mZ9vB8

./. • Iron • Walter Dorwin Teague
   http://bit.ly/2mtaN5i
   http://bit.ly/2Dp3Prd
   http://bit.ly/2noFK3P

RUPPELWERKE • Table Clock • Marianne Brandt
   https://mo.ma/3esjpoM
   https://bit.ly/3enG1a5

SCHOTT • Tea Pot • Wilhelm Wagenfeld
   http://bit.ly/2Du8QCF
   http://bit.ly/2DYdqX2

./. • Anglepoise Lamp • George Carwardine
http://bit.ly/2EYCTyU
http://bit.ly/2DuRzJP
http://bit.ly/1BQ6YXy

ZIPPO • Lighter • George G. Blaisdell
http://bit.ly/2DqORB2
http://bit.ly/2DmQSOr
http://bit.ly/2DvTjCE

DR. G. SEIBT • VE 301 W • Walter Maria Kersting
http://bit.ly/2DnqHHf
http://bit.ly/2lEbnOJ
http://bit.ly/2mwZXv6

WESTERN ELECTRIC • 302 Phone • Henry Dreyfuss
http://bit.ly/1PdHsco
http://bit.ly/2DAKCpw
http://bit.ly/2G3JuJJ

HOMER LAUGHLIN CHINA CO. • Fiestaware • Frederick Hurten Rhead
http://bit.ly/2rrvm9R
http://bit.ly/2mWfjfx
http://bit.ly/2FZVlIH

KODAK • Bantam Special • Walter Dorwin Teague
http://bit.ly/2BjUFKw
http://bit.ly/2GoATaJ
http://bit.ly/2DnhIWS

RIMOWA • Aluminum Luggage • Richard Morszeck
http://bit.ly/2EYDhNS
http://bit.ly/2DwExum
http://bit.ly/2DmdKop

MINOX • Riga Camera • Walter Zapp
http://bit.ly/2DvJHrt
http://bit.ly/2mXrsjD
http://bit.ly/2FZVGLt

SWANN-MORTON • Scalpel • unknown
http://bit.ly/2BizqZN
http://bit.ly/2G3lMNp

BIALETTI • Moka Express • Alfonso Bialetti
http://bit.ly/1OZCtt1
http://cnn.it/1UbYB63

VOLKSWAGEN • Beetle • Ferdinand Porsche
https://bit.ly/3enqln4
https://bit.ly/3cotEsu
https://bit.ly/3epw6R**a**

VIPP • Pedal Bin • Holger Nielsen
https://bit.ly/2Vt6oUM
https://bit.ly/2VClKEU
https://bit.ly/2VaO3v8

EMERSON RADIO & PHONOGRAPH CORP. • Patriot Radio • Norman Bel Geddes

https://bit.ly/3bdCoBj
https://bit.ly/2K8OFLz
https://bit.ly/2K8ORuh

S. T. DUPONT • Lighter • unknown

http://bit.ly/2mYXNXQ
http://bit.ly/2mWMoYo
http://bit.ly/2BhWIib

KODAK • Brownie Six-20 • unknown

http://bit.ly/1NxrQuM
http://bit.ly/1zAtulF
http://www.brownie.camera

HOWARD MILLER • Ball Clock • George Nelson

http://bit.ly/2DX2nNQ
http://bit.ly/2mZ7Pby
http://bit.ly/2mYKANR

MOVADO • Museum Watch • Nathan George Horwitt

http://bit.ly/2Du1bEz
http://bit.ly/2DWYRTF

CITROËN • 2CV • Flaminio Bertoni

http://bit.ly/2DzD9ql
http://bit.ly/2rmRYYW
http://bit.ly/2mYOiqO

BUSH • TV 22 • unknown

http://bbc.in/2GoBZmR
http://bit.ly/2mYOfv8
http://bit.ly/2DWIu9z

WEBER • Grill • George A. Stephen

http://bit.ly/2Dr8U6a
http://s.si.edu/1q3IklC
http://bit.ly/2kKX77V

BIC • Cristal Pen • Décolletage Plastique

http://bit.ly/1ulHVYO
http://bit.ly/2EZ7DQo

PAVONI • Europiccola • unknown

http://bit.ly/2DwE8YP
http://bit.ly/2EYEgO4

BAUSCH & LOMB • Ray Ban Wayfarer • Raymond Stegeman

http://bit.ly/2Bj5TyQ
http://bit.ly/2DwwEoW
http://bit.ly/2Dp2GzM

FENDER • Stratocaster • Leo Fender, Bill Carson, George Fullerton, Freddie Tavares

http://bit.ly/2DUDu5h
http://bit.ly/2bH5RtZ
http://bit.ly/2GoEqWx

ESGE • Zauberstab • Acton Bjørn

http://bit.ly/2DvT7TS

**LONDON TRANSPORT • Routemaster • A.M. Durrant,
Colin Curtis, Douglas Scott**

http://bit.ly/2F2byM9

http://bit.ly/2Dv2keS

http://bit.ly/2mWh1xt

**ROSTI • Margrethe Mixing Bowl • Sigvard
Bernadotte, Acton Bjørn**

http://bit.ly/2DW9GFs

http://bit.ly/2mWpKyF

http://bit.ly/2mYXNHu

PIAGGIO • Vespa • Corradino d'Ascanio

http://bit.ly/2BirHL0

BRAUN • SK4 • Hans Gugelot, Dieter Rams

http://bit.ly/2mZqzYl

http://bit.ly/R98AN2

**LOUIS POULSEN • Artichoke Lamp • Poul
Henningsen**

https://ind.pn/23W8wB0

http://bit.ly/1O2nF8j

http://bit.ly/1V2KNcs

ROLODEX • Address File • Hildaur Neilsen

http://bit.ly/2DwFDXo

http://bit.ly/2DsYqmS

BRAUN • T3 • Dieter Rams

http://bit.ly/2Dpf4zH

http://on.ft.com/2G3nJJJ

http://bit.ly/2F1ivNF

MONO • A • Peter Raacke

http://bit.ly/2DtvdIn

http://bit.ly/2n3bo2b

THOMAS • TC100 • Nick Roericht

http://bit.ly/2rtHhE2

http://bit.ly/2DBohFm

http://ubm.io/2mYP7jo

SONY • 8-301 • unknown

http://bit.ly/2kuR84F

http://bit.ly/2GoA4yv

http://bit.ly/2DzSWpO

VITRA • Panton Chair • Verner Panton

http://bit.ly/2DuZypp

https://ind.pn/1yJGgAl

http://bit.ly/2DxQm4o

OHIO ART COMPANY • Etch A Sketch • André
Cassagnes
http://bit.ly/1TqLvjt
http://bit.ly/2mWrRT7
http://ti.me/2DwxSk2

FLOS • Arco • Achille & Pier Giacomo Castiglioni
http://bit.ly/2FoP2ml
http://bit.ly/2DkDSJ5
https://ind.pn/2EYFTLG

BULOVA • Accutron • unknown
http://bit.ly/2mZcx8u
http://bit.ly/2DULzqr
http://bit.ly/2DWKMVY

IBM • Selectric • Eliot Noyes
http://bit.ly/2DAoBnQ
http://engt.co/2DWEozB
http://bit.ly/2DUzsd4

KIKKOMAN • Soy Sauce Bottle • Kenji Ekuan
http://bit.ly/2DtbYil
http://mo.ma/2EZK2Pf
http://nyti.ms/2mYZ9C4

BRAUN • MX 32 • Gerd Alfred Müller, Robert Oberheim
http://bit.ly/2DvVAOc

BRAUN • Sixtant SM 31 • Hans Gugelot, Gerd A. Müller
http://bit.ly/2G1tp7f

HAVAIANAS • Flip-Flop Sandals • Robert Fraser
http://bit.ly/2DVSFv2
http://on.ft.com/2rntLCo

VIEW-MASTER • Model G • unknown
http://bit.ly/2BiYXBY
http://bit.ly/2rwUoob
http://bit.ly/1RnUDm6

KODAK • Carousel • Hans Gugelot, Reinhold Hacker
http://nyti.ms/2noPN8L
http://bit.ly/2Dtw1Np
http://bit.ly/2DvUT7u

BRIONVEGA • Cubo Radio • Richard Sapper, Marco
Zanuso
http://bit.ly/1npiGaE
http://bit.ly/2Du5glP

PENTEL • Sign Pen (Fiber Tip Pen) • Yukio Horie
http://bit.ly/2BgQBut
http://bit.ly/2BjNL7Z

BRIONVEGA • Algol 11• Richard Sapper, Marco Zanuso
http://bit.ly/2mZznoG
http://bit.ly/2DpTsn3
http://bit.ly/2mYEDBC

OLIVETTI • Programma 101 • Mario Bellini

http://bit.ly/1sRr8DQ

http://bit.ly/2rwWo1d

ARTICLOI PLASTICI ELETTRICI • Stackable Melamine Dinnerware • Lella + Massimo Vignelli

https://mo.ma/2wKiSxx

https://bit.ly/3ersZZ3

https://bit.ly/34KC6iX

O-LUCE • Spider • Joe Colombo

http://bit.ly/2F2dlRn

http://bit.ly/2mYOQwP

STUDIO M • Bulb Lamp • Ingo Maurer

http://bit.ly/2DxSaKI

http://mo.ma/2DrhA8s

http://bit.ly/2DAOA1o

FISKARS • O-Series • Olof Bäckström

http://bit.ly/2ru2D3Y

http://bit.ly/2mXAFsd

KODAK • Instamatic • Kenneth Grange

http://bit.ly/2o8XpEh

http://bit.ly/2DzLwCU

http://bit.ly/2FoP1zm

GDB • Mineral Water Bottle • Günter Kupetz

http://bit.ly/2mWvvMN

http://bit.ly/2DuTIFe

http://bit.ly/2DWOJtM

VLM • Light Switch • Achille Castiglioni

http://bit.ly/2DlB2Uh

ROSENTHAL • Tea Pot • Walter Gropius

http://bit.ly/2BiCxAX

OLIVETTI • Valentine • Perry A. King, Ettore Sottsass

http://bit.ly/2mYaMJg

http://bit.ly/2p9d8qm

DESIGN M • Wall Storage Panel • Dorothée Becker

https://bit.ly/2REUaWj

https://on.ft.com/3evgR9A

https://bit.ly/2VfX8mG

BRAUN • HLD 4 • Dieter Rams

http://bit.ly/2DV5mpZ

http://bit.ly/2G1dzte

VILLEROY&BOCH • La Boule • Helen von Boch, Federigo Fabbrini

https://bit.ly/3ctE4XT

https://bit.ly/2Vwhs24

https://bit.ly/2RH7pWM

POLAROID • SX-70 • Henry Dreyfuss

http://bit.ly/2DWVonY

http://bit.ly/2Dv23bh

http://bit.ly/2G1qBH5

WEGA • TV 3050 • Esslinger Design
http://bit.ly/2DnoM5K

ARTEMIDE • Tizio • Richard Sapper
http://bit.ly/2G1dHJe
http://mo.ma/2EZIBRo

FLOS • Parentesi • Achille Castiglioni, Pio Manzù
http://bit.ly/2G3rcrJ
http://bit.ly/2F1swua
http://bit.ly/2DwHiMb

OLIVETTI • Divisumma 18 • Mario Bellini
http://bit.ly/2EZdu7W
http://bit.ly/2mZoLLV
http://bit.ly/2mXl8JA

CINI & NILS • Cuboluce • Franco Bettonica, Mario Melocchi
http://bit.ly/2DuVSEZ
http://bit.ly/2EZlwga

DENNERT & PAPE • Aristo M65 • unknown
http://bit.ly/2no5oFy
http://bit.ly/2BjuNyh
http://bit.ly/2FoSJsA

BIC • Lighter • Louis Lepoix
http://bit.ly/2BgT9sx

LIP • Dark Master • Roger Tallon
http://bit.ly/2FoXNoc
http://bit.ly/2DqyAvN

SINCLAIR • Black Watch • Clive Sinclair
http://bit.ly/2FoXPoQ
http://bit.ly/2DvYna8
http://bit.ly/2mYRvHZ

BANG + OLUFSEN • Beomaster 2400 • Jacob Jensen
http://bit.ly/2Foytav
http://bit.ly/2rwXCbh
http://bit.ly/2no5EEw

STELTON • Thermal Carafe • Erik Magnusson
http://bit.ly/2mYXNHu
http://bit.ly/2G3S1MK

ARTEMIDE • Sintesi • Ernesto Gismondi
http://bit.ly/2EYllxh

WEGA • Concept 51K • frogdesign, Hartmut Esslinger
http://bit.ly/2DwAcYi
http://bit.ly/2rvrJQm
http://bit.ly/2DuMqAH

FLOS • Frisbi • Achille Castiglioni
http://bit.ly/2DomP9f

SIGG • Water Bottle • Kurt Zimmerli
http://bit.ly/2DUK0aE
http://bit.ly/2mWTXOa

MAGLIGHT • Flashlight • Anthony Maglica
http://bit.ly/2FXTiVs
http://nyp.st/1GBVZs6

CARRERA • Sunglasses • Porsche Design
http://bit.ly/2DBfmqD

JCDECAUX • Public Toilet "S.P.E.A." • Jean-Claude
Decaux
http://bit.ly/2mZtIY9
http://bit.ly/2G3Q6b1

SONY • Walkman • Sony Design Center
http://bit.ly/1ql43Eq
http://ti.me/1lx1HMK
http://bit.ly/1T6P2n1

BRAUN • Micron Plus • Roland Ullmann
http://bit.ly/2F0RzNW
http://bit.ly/2mXDCsN
http://bit.ly/2DpXETP

LEATHERMAN • Pocket Survival Tool • Timothe S.
Leatherman
http://bit.ly/2Dtb858
http://tcrn.ch/2Drj9TS

SWATCH • Jelly Fish • unknown
http://tcrn.ch/2mWjYy3
http://bit.ly/2DBfTsD
http://bit.ly/2mZu7K9

APPLE • Macintosh • Steve Jobs, Jerry Manock,
Terry Oyama
http://bit.ly/2DTqDQJ
http://bit.ly/2l9xvjB
http://bit.ly/1avfNQ4

ALESSI • Bollitore • Richard Sapper
http://bit.ly/TX5xbC

MOTOROLA • DynaTAC 8000x • unknown
http://bit.ly/1FmwHfx
http://ti.me/TkQngH

OAKLEY • Factory Pilot Eyeshades • James Jannard
https://bit.ly/2XDU4lF
https://bit.ly/2Vyinin
https://bit.ly/3etmrsH

BRAUN • AB 312 vsl • Dietrich Lubs
http://bit.ly/2mZc2fm

ARTEMIDE • Tolomeo • Michele De Lucchi, Giancarlo
Fassina
http://bit.ly/2DUWosJ
http://bit.ly/2DxUtNS

EDDING • Marker 3000 • Jens Plewa
http://bit.ly/2mYCXIm
http://bit.ly/2DYYojT

BRAUN • ET66 • Dietrich Lubs, Dieter Rams
http://bit.ly/2G1AtRj
http://bit.ly/2DUMjMo

FLOS • Ara Lamp • Philippe Starck
http://bit.ly/2n12ouh

SONY • Walkman Sports • Sony Design Center
http://bit.ly/1ql43Eq
http://bit.ly/2G1ch1f

NINTENDO • Game Boy • Gunpei Yokoi
https://bit.ly/2VwK3UJ
https://on.ft.com/2K6pFoi
https://bit.ly/2XFpfgz

OXO • Peeler • Smart Design
http://bit.ly/1jTDjIk
http://s.si.edu/2Dv8lZo

ALESSI • Juicy Salif • Philippe Starck
http://bit.ly/2rpEBHF

DYSON • DC01 • James Dyson
http://bit.ly/2DUJhYz

ALESSI • Anna G • Alessandro Mendini
http://bit.ly/2DX8f9R
http://on.ft.com/2G2LxxI

APPLE • iMac • Jony Ive
http://apple-history.com/imac
http://bit.ly/2DUiHP8
http://bit.ly/1avfNQ4

MOULTON • Spaceframe Bicycle • Alex Moulton
http://bit.ly/2BiNEJZ

3M • Palm V • IDEO
http://bit.ly/2DV982D
http://bit.ly/2mYWzer
http://bit.ly/2DnBXU8

MUJI • CD Player • Naoto Fukasawa
http://bit.ly/2DvZeYk
http://bit.ly/2Bke9ii

NOKIA • 8210 • unknown
http://cnet.co/2DWiICm
http://bit.ly/2BiokRr
http://bit.ly/2BioqbL

APPLE • Cube • Apple Design Team
http://bit.ly/2GoMruB
http://engt.co/2pogTdh

APPLE • iPod • Jony Ive
http://bit.ly/1ECVjC1
http://cnet.co/2BkeaTo
http://apple-history.com/ipod

KARTELL • Louis Ghost • Philippe Starck
http://bit.ly/2DpiTEW
http://bit.ly/2Fosxyj
http://bit.ly/2Bjxfot

APPLE • iPhone • Apple Design Team
http://bit.ly/1vx2XJf
http://bit.ly/1TrEYGJ
http://bit.ly/1ROBhwl

OLPC • Laptop for Children • Yves Béhar
https://nyti.ms/2Rlierl
https://bit.ly/2XDDp1A
https://bit.ly/2xrrzx8

APPLE • Magic Mouse • Apple Design Team
http://bit.ly/2DtgP33
http://bit.ly/2nom4Mi

DYSON • Air Multiplier • James Dyson
http://ti.me/2DUj2Bo
http://bit.ly/2mWovzC
http://bit.ly/15VBWWo

O2COOL • Water Filter Bottle "Bobble" • Karim Rashid
https://bit.ly/2ygz2Pw
https://bit.ly/3esZjuE
https://bit.ly/3bj87Be

NEST • Thermostat • Fred Bould
https://bit.ly/2KfFZmt
https://bit.ly/3copS24
https://bit.ly/2KblokQ

LITTLE SUN • Solar-Powered Lamp • Olafur Eliasson, Frederik Ottesen
https://bit.ly/2VeNyA8
https://mo.ma/2VaQOg6
https://bit.ly/2wJUR9H